DUXFORD

1940

About the Author

Fascinated by the Battle of Britain since childhood, Dilip Sarkar remains both moved and inspired by the story of Churchill's fabled 'Few', those young airmen who stood between freedom and a Britain dominated by Nazi Germany. Since the 1970s he has met and interviewed more Battle of Britain pilots than any other historian. He has researched the subject thoroughly and has published over twenty books the only biographical works formally endorsed by the families of both Group Captain Sir Douglas Bader and Air Vice-Marshal Johnnie Johnson. In 2003, Dilip was made an MBE for services to aviation history, and he was elected to the Fellowship of the Royal Historical Society in 2006. He lives in Worcester.

DUXFORD 1940

A BATTLE OF BRITAIN BASE AT WAR

Dilip Sarkar MBE FRHistS

AMBERLEY

First published 2009

Amberley Publishing
Cirencester Road, Chalford,
Stroud, Gloucestershire, GL6 8PE

www.amberley-books.com

British Library Cataloguing in Publication Data.
A catalogue record for this book is available from the British Library.

ISBN 978 1 84868 213 9

Typesetting and Origination by Diagraf (www.diagraf.net)
Printed in Great Britain

For my children, Simon, James & Hannah

Introduction

The name Duxford will forever be synonymous with two things: the Spitfire fighter aircraft, for it was here that the RAF took delivery of the first operational example in 1938, and the epic Battle of Britain two years later, when Duxford performed a crucial role as No 12 Group's main Sector Station. For those with knowledge of those now far off but dramatic times, certain personalities will also forever be associated with this hallowed ground: the legless Douglas Bader, 'Woody' Woodhall, Brian Lane, George 'Grumpy' Unwin, Douglas Blackwood, the list goes ever on. Moreover, in 1969, Duxford, still then an RAF station, was one of the venues at which the *Battle of Britain* film was shot. For those lucky enough to have peeped through the wire, what an incredible sight there was to behold during that particular post war summer: Heinkels, 'Messerschmitts' (actually, Spanish built Hispano-Bouchons), Spitfires and Hurricanes all lined up together! Today Duxford is well-known throughout the world as the Imperial War Museum's working airfield, and widely regarded as Europe's premier aviation museum. Every year thousands of visitors flock to the venue, and at summer air shows experience the sight and sound of vintage WW2 aircraft – amongst them the unforgettable and still iconic Spitfire. On the ground are veterans too, now aged pensioners who, in our Finest Hour, once soared aloft from Duxford's grass to engage the Luftwaffe. Others worked on the ground, in various supporting roles, and were bombed there; it is an honour and privilege to meet these men and women, and I am fortunate indeed to have known many of them during my lifetime.

Today, we who were not born in 1940 can only imagine what it was really like back then, but we can at least refer to both the written and photographic record. After the war many celebrated RAF fighter pilots either published auto-biographies or, as in the case of Douglas Bader, had books written about them. Paul Brickhill was an Australian Spitfire pilot who turned his hand after the war to writing about derring-do from the Hitler war: *The Dambusters, The Great Escape*, and, of course, Bader's story in *Reach for the Sky* all flowed from his talented pen. The latter became an international best seller and a cinema classic of the same name starring Kenneth Moore. There were also titles lesser known to the public, and largely forgotten today by all but we 'buffs', such as Squadron Leader 'BJ Ellan's *Spitfire! The Experiences of a Fighter Pilot*, published in 1942. 'Ellan' was actually a pseudonym for 19 Squadron's Commanding Officer, Squadron Leader Brian Lane DFC, who was reported Missing in Action during 1942. Earlier that year his book was published, punctuated with such terrific contemporary words as 'prang', 'types', 'wizard' and 'Huns' (see Bibliography).

DUXFORD 1940

Amongst the colourful characters who served at Duxford during the Battle of Britain, and as recounted by Brickhill in *Reach for the Sky*, was Group Captain 'Woody' Woodhall, who was the Station Commander and 'boss' Fighter Controller. Woodhall was an amazing man who served as a soldier, sailor and an airman. In the film *Reach for the Sky*, Woodhall's memorable part was played by Howard Marion-Crawford, but surprisingly 'Woody' did not cash in on his new found fame and recognition by publishing his story. Fortunately Group Captain Woodhall did write his memoirs, appropriately titled 'Soldier, Sailor, Airman Too', but, surprisingly, these remain unpublished to this day. I am therefore indebted to 'Woody's' son, Martin Woodhall, for having provided me with a copy over a decade ago, the Battle of Britain section of which I am now able to publish here, with Martin's kind permission, to introduce the reader to Battle of Britain Duxford – and who better to do that than the Station Commander himself?

Of those indelible days, Woody wrote:

In my new posting I found myself to be second-in-command to Wing Commander 'Pingo' Lester. My official title was Squadron Leader Flying Ops, and, in addition to being administration officer, I was made responsible for the development of the Fighter Control System and the training of the Operations Room crews.

My biggest administrative task was to plan the evacuation from the Station of all married families, which would take place as soon as mobilisation for war was ordered. As this entailed the arranging of transport by the most economical means for all the wives and children to their chosen destination, it was no mean task.

At this time there were two squadrons on the Station, Nos 19 and 66, both armed with the new Spitfire Mk I. Squadron Leader Cozens commanded the former, and Squadron Leader Fullergood, an old friend from Netheravon days, the latter. Their Mk I Spitfires, owing to the fact that the airscrew was fixed, had poor take-off performance because acceleration was poor until airborne; this was resolved, however, through first the introduction of the De Havilland two pitch airscrew, later the Rotol variable pitch airscrew, making the Spitfire a magnificent aircraft in every way.

It was at Duxford that I first met Air Vice-Marshal Trafford Leigh-Mallory, who was then our AOC with his No 12 Group Headquarters at Hucknall in Nottinghamshire. 'LM' was a true gentleman and a most capable and efficient commander respected and esteemed by all ranks that served under him. In my opinion he was one of the great leaders who deservedly reached the top in the last war; his death in a flying accident whilst en route to India, to take over Supreme Command from Mountbatten in 1944, was a great loss to his country and the service. I also lost a good friend.

A notable character at Duxford was Warrant Officer Whiting, the Station Warrant Officer. When I first took over my job I was greeted by Whiting, who said, with a beaming smile, "I don't suppose you remember me, Sir?"

I replied, "Your face is familiar and I would say that you were taught to salute in the Royal Marines?"

"That's right, Sir, last time I saw you was in 1917. You were Orderly Officer at Forton Barracks, and I was a Drummer Boy. You had to witness my punishment when I was given 'half a dozen of the best' by the Drum Major for being caught smoking."

Whiting proved to be one of the best disciplinary Warrant Officers I ever served with in the RAF and was a tower of strength to me as the number of station personnel increased rapidly as war approached.

The Fighter Control System was rapidly developing. The Observer Corps already existed for visual and sound reporting, and the RDF chain (now called radar) was being quickly established. Joint control of our defences was agreed so that the AA guns and searchlights were co-ordinated with Fighter Control. At the top, Fighter Command and Anti-aircraft Command were closely integrated, and at Sector level, AA and Searchlight Control Officers were established in the same Operations Rooms as the RAF and worked closely with the Fighter Control Officers there. It was at Sector level, Duxford being a Sector Station, that Fighter Control became a personal affair. From the Sector Station the Controller was in direct communication with the fighter pilots by R/T (radio telephone). With the development and installation of VHF (very high frequency) R/T just before the outbreak of war, the distances at which one could communicate increased tremendously.

When I arrived at Duxford there was only a skeleton Operations Room crew in charge of the Signals Warrant Officer, and controlling was shared between the Station Commander, the two Squadron Commanders and me. The most important job was to train sufficient personnel to man the Operations Room on a 24-hour basis. The RAFVR, which in peacetime was only on a part time basis, provided the first trainees, but when the WAAF came into being we were delighted to get girls as plotters. One of the first RAFVR officers to join was an old friend, KK Horn; I had last seen him in 1930 at Hornchurch when, as the first Commanding Officer of 54 Squadron in the Kaiser's War, he had presented a trophy to the re-formed 54 Squadron. I was astonished and delighted when he walked into my office, wearing only a single ring on his sleeve, but with an impressive display of medal ribbons on his chest.

In May or June we were given another task: the preliminary training of young National Servicemen, which was most ably carried out by Warrant Officer Whiting. To accommodate this influx, Nissen huts were hurriedly erected. About this time a 'satellite' airfield was completed, with Nissen huts, at Fowlmere, about three miles away, to accommodate one of the Duxford squadrons.

The two squadrons were, of course, always training hard on their new Spitfires, and even in those pre-war days, one flight, known as the 'Battle Flight', was always at 'Readiness'. By June, night flying training was in full swing, and one night 66 Squadron had three pilots airborne, practising night formation, and another young pilot on his first night solo in a Spitfire, when what was known in Cambridgeshire as a 'Hah' materialised. This 'Hah' was a kind of thin cloud with a base of about 300 feet that could appear very suddenly, and in a few minutes cover the whole of the flat plain. Before I could bring the aircraft in to land, this low cloud had blotted out the flare path, so I ordered the pilots to land at Northolt, where I knew a flare path was laid out ready. The formation leader acknowledged the order, but I could get no response from Bob Oxspring, who was on his first night solo. All we could do was fire rockets at intervals to show where the aerodrome was. I went onto the aerodrome and heard an aircraft circling overhead. Suddenly Bob appeared below the cloud, obviously sighted the flare path and decided to land. Visibility below the cloud was very poor, and Bob hurriedly lowered his flaps and undercarriage, but his speed was so high that he touched down about a hundred yards from the end of the landing 'T' and, still travelling fast, disappeared through the boundary hedge into a ploughed field. By the time I had jumped into my car and, followed by the fire tender and ambulance, reached what I feared would be a rather nasty crash, Bob had taxied out of the ploughed field; I met him taxiing back along the main road! I sent the fire tender and ambulance back, and held up main road traffic until the main gate at the aerodrome was reached. There we struck a problem – the gateposts were too narrow for a Spitfire to be pushed through and, additionally, there was a solid cast iron GPO red pillar-box alongside the outer gatepost. Having parked my car, I arrived back at the gate to find an enthusiastic bunch of pilots trying to push the pillar-box over using an old sports car as a bulldozer! I stopped this and pointed out that by bearing down on the port wing we could lift the starboard wing over the gatepost and letter-box. The amazing thing was that the only damage to the Spitfire was a dent or two to the aluminium undercarriage fairing. Bob Oxspring, who is now a Group Captain and has earned high decorations in the war, is the son of an equally distinguished father, affectionately known in the First World War as 'Oxo' and who, with KK Horn, served in the original No 54 Squadron, RFC.

Shortly before war was declared, mobilisation of reserves and auxiliaries was ordered, and Duxford received its quota, including the first of the WAAF. These girls, all volunteers, were grand types, and were a very welcome addition to our strength. They were extremely keen to learn their jobs, and became efficient as well as decorative in a very short time.

The first detachment of WAAF reported as soon as wives and families had been evacuated. This evacuation, thanks to our early planning, was completed in 48 hours, and the WAAF took over the Airmen's Married Quarters, six girls to a house. I allotted an Officer's Married Quarter to the WAAF officers as a mess and sleeping quarters. The first girls to report had been issued with a blue Burberry and a beret as their only uniform. They were plotters, clerks and MT drivers, and had received a little training in their trades, but it fell to the unfailing Warrant Officer Whiting to give them their basic disciplinary and parade ground work. As soon as their proper uniforms arrived these girls were a credit to the Air Force, and were so good looking that an officer from Group Headquarters, after seeing the WAAF plotters in the Operations Room, referred to them as "Woody's Beauty Chorus!"

Just prior to mobilisation, No 611 Auxiliary Squadron came to Duxford for their annual training, and upon full mobilisation being ordered, remained. Their CO was an MP, and on outbreak of war he handed over command to the senior flight commander, James McComb. James, who retired at the end of the war as a group captain, went on to lead the Squadron with distinction during the Battle of Britain.

The declaration of war found us reasonably prepared, inasmuch as we had sufficient air-raid shelters, and we all possessed gas masks and were familiar with their use. The Fighter Operations Room had sufficient trained staff (of both sexes) to provide round the clock service. In readiness for bombing attacks, the aircraft were dispersed around the aerodrome perimeter, dispersal huts for ground and aircrews had been built. We only used the hangars for aircraft undergoing inspection or repair.

The Squadrons, in those early days, had very little rest. From before dawn they were either flying on patrols over the coastwise convoys passing up and down the East coast, carrying out flying training or at 'Readiness' at their dispersals. Night flying training was carried on as soon as dusk fell. For forward bases we used Coltishall and Horsham St Faith on the Norfolk coast. These aerodromes were completed so far as the landing area was concerned, but the buildings were still under construction, so we sent the convoy patrol flight or squadron there daily. This entailed taking off from Duxford before dawn and returning after dark in order to maintain the convoy patrol throughout the daylight hours. The boredom, long hours with insufficient sleep, no action and no leave, soon began to tell on the pilots. This fatigue showed itself rather alarmingly when one of the flight commanders, leading his formation in to land, actually fell asleep when on the final approach. I was watching at the time, and it seemed that the Flight Commander would lead his Flight to crash into a hangar. The two pilots in formation realised something was wrong, and broke away, but the Flight Commander (who was a tough Australian affectionately nicknamed 'Granny') only awoke when his wheels hit the ground and, was lucky enough, by use of full throttle, to just clear the hangar and go round again. When I greeted him as he climbed out of the aircraft he nearly broke down, and was almost asleep on his feet.

I felt so strongly about this fatigue that the boys were being subjected to, that I immediately wrote a very strong letter to the AOC, pointing out that the rigid state of readiness should be relaxed and provision made for regular leave and recreation, otherwise we were asking for accidents. I got Pingo Lester to sign, as Station Commander, and flew up to Hucknall to deliver the letter myself. Leigh-Mallory saw me at once, and I am afraid that I rather forgot myself, and thumped his table when he said he could not alter orders from Fighter Command, and I said something to the effect that we were wearing the pilots out by sheer fatigue. I never admired 'LM' more than I did when, ignoring my distressing lack of discipline and manners, he said, "Woody, believe me I have tried already to persuade the C-in-C to relax the boys, but I'll try again now." With that he picked up the scrambler phone to Fighter Command. The outcome was that the state of readiness was relaxed considerably so that pilots were given 48 hours leave at reasonable intervals.

The sad part was that when we landed back at Duxford, Jimmy Copley, the Station Adjutant, had flown up with me as passenger, we were greeted by Pingo Lester with the dreadful news that Jimmy's son had been killed in a flying accident at Wittering that afternoon – it was thought that fatigue was the cause.

After war was declared the numbers at Duxford increased rapidly, 222 Squadron, commanded by Tubby Mermagen, arrived equipped with Blenheim fighters, but almost at once were re-armed with Spitfires. Geoffrey Stephenson took over command of 19 Squadron and towards the end of 1939, Rupert Leigh, another old friend, took over 66 Squadron.

One day, Douglas Bader flew over from Central Flying School, in a Hurricane. I was delighted and amazed to see him. He was in terrific form, and as it happened the AOC also came to visit us. I introduced Douglas to the AOC, and over lunch, Douglas used all his considerable charm in persuading Leigh-Mallory to take him into one of his operational fighter squadrons. After lunch, with the AOC watching, Douglas put on a most finished display of aerobatics, and this finally decided 'LM'. Douglas was posted almost at once to No 19 Squadron, under his old friend and term-mate from Cranwell, Geoffrey Stephenson. Douglas, although only a flying officer then, impressed us all with his terrific personality, and his amazing keenness and drive. I have never known anyone to equal him. Flying was his supreme passion, and his enthusiasm infected us all.

As a spectator I was intrigued to see the impact that Douglas had on the AOC – and vice-versa. Air Vice-Marshal and Flying Officer – rank did not enter into it – they were two of a kind: born leaders. Both men were respected by all, and were affectionately esteemed by most. Their attraction for each other was immediate, and their friendship was, I am sure, established at that first meeting. Until then I had not seen Douglas since his crash in 1930, and, in his maturity (he was about 30 when he joined us at Duxford) he appealed to me very strongly. Such was his zest for living and flying that one forgot his artificial legs. He ignored them, and so did everyone else. His prowess at golf and squash racquets was such that very few people on the Station were a match for him at either game, and, of course, as a fighter pilot he was superb. Douglas had made an intimate study of the fighter tactics developed by famous pilots like McCudden, Ball and Bishop in the First War, and was a great believer in the advantages of making correct use of the sun, and first gaining superior height.

Certain stereotyped forms of attack had been laid down in peacetime by Fighter Command, but these were, in my opinion, only valuable as a sort of air drill which trained the pilots to react rapidly to their leaders' instructions. As I saw it, my job as Sector Controller was to vector the Fighter Leader on a course and to a height which would place him above, and up sun of the enemy, and keep him informed of the enemy's position, course and speed, as accurately as possible from the information we had on the Operations Table. As soon as our Fighter Leader spotted the enemy, it was over to him.

In those early days radar information was not very accurate, particularly regarding height and numbers of aircraft and, of course, there was a time lag of several minutes before the information reached the Sector Operations Room. The Sector Controller therefore had to use intelligent guesswork in order to direct his fighters on an intercepting course and also to position them up-sun of and above the enemy.

To begin with, the Operations Tables in No 12 Group only extended to the North bank of the Thames, and enemy plots were only passed to us when they reached that point. In No 11 Group, however, enemy plots were received whilst the enemy was still over France! Fighter Command Operations Room, of course, had the whole picture, but in my opinion there was insufficient liaison between 11 and 12 Groups. Luckily Victor Beamish, the Station Commander at North Weald, was a good friend of mine and so I extended our Operations Table as far south as St Omer, in France. Immediately North Weald was informed of enemy activity we kept the tie-line telephone open, and plots were passed from North Weald to Duxford. In that way we obtained earlier warning, but in spite of this, we were frequently scrambled too late, because we were not allowed to fly over 11 Group's territory, unless asked for by 11 Group. It was frustrating to see an enemy raid plotted on our board, obviously going for a target in 11 Group, then to wait on the ground with the pilots in their cockpits for 15 – 20 minutes, and finally be scrambled too late to get into the fight.

Situated as Duxford was, about 60 miles north of the Thames, our fighters could be over Kent at 25,000 feet, 15 minutes after take-off. Under Douglas Bader's leadership, first of all three squadrons, and later five, would be airborne, and climbing as a Wing on an intercepting course in less than six minutes from the scramble order. On the few occasions when the Duxford Wing was asked for in time, Douglas Bader more than justified his theories, as the Station 'scoreboard' showed. This was rather like a cricket scoreboard, giving details of each squadron's tally of enemy aircraft destroyed, probably destroyed or damaged.

In order to maintain a close liaison between aircraft, AA guns and searchlights, each Sector Operations Room was in direct contact with the appropriate AA brigade. The Senior Gun Control Officer was Captain Walter Kester, who in civilian life was (and is) a well-known lawyer in Cambridge. Walter was a great character with an impish sense of humour, as the following story will show:

We had, at the time of the first WAAFs arrival, a certain elderly RAF type, who joined as an Ops B officer. I will merely call him 'A'. Now 'A', who was balding and with prominent bags under his eyes, thought himself rather a devil with the ladies, but unfortunately the ladies did not agree. He went on a short leave, and on his return we noticed that he had freshly healed scars under each eye, which he said was the result of flying glass in a car accident. Walter Kester whispered to me, "The blighter has had his face lifted!" About a fortnight later 'A' appeared after another visit to London, looking surprisingly youthful. For some time we could not account for it, until about 2 am, when things were very quiet in the Operations Room, that Walter Kester called across to me, "I've discovered the secret of eternal youth, Woody!" and, leaning forward, plucked a toupee from the wretched man's head, to the delight of the whole Ops Room crew! 'A' got himself posted to another station shortly after that; we often wondered if his face-lift and toupee had their required effect elsewhere!

When Christmas 1939 arrived, the increased numbers on the Station stretched our cooking facilities to the limit. However, by dint of our WAAFs boiling the Christmas puddings in the coppers in the billets in the old Married Quarters, augmenting our cookhouse with field kitchens, to which access was only possible through the mud and snow by means of duckboards, everyone agreed that the Christmas dinner was more than adequate.

Duxford was the Fighter Station chosen by the BBC for the Commonwealth-wide broadcast that went round the world just prior to the King's Christmas speech. As luck would have it, we had at least one man or woman from every Commonwealth country on our strength, and each, in turn, gave a brief message to their countrymen at home.

On 1 January 1940, I was promoted to Wing Commander and to my sorrow, was posted as Senior Personnel Staff Officer to No 20 Technical Training Group at Market Drayton. This was, to me, an irksome chair borne job, so that when in the middle of March 1940, I was posted back to Duxford as Station Commander, my joy cannot be imagined. Most of my old friends were there, but Geoffrey Stephenson had taken over command of 19 Squadron from Cozens, and Rupert Leigh had succeeded Fullergood in command of 66. Douglas Bader was still there and soon promoted to be a flight commander in Tubby Mermagen's 222 Squadron.

The 'Phoney War' was still ongoing, and our time still fully occupied with convoy patrols, night-flying training, battle training and long periods of readiness. About this time England was split into Regions, each with its own Regional Commissioner, who was the King's Representative and who would act as Governor of his Region in the event of an emergency. Our Regional Commissioner for East Anglia was Sir Will Spens, the Master of Trinity College, Cambridge. It was conceivable that, with the expected heavy bombing, possible invasion or national calamity, the control normally exercised by Parliament from London would fail through disrupted communications, or even the obliteration of London and the Houses of Parliament. In this event, plans were laid for each region to carry on the fight, controlling its own distribution, civil defence, medical services and its armed services. The RAF Liaison Officer was Air Vice-Marshal Norman McEwen, affectionately known to us all as 'Uncle Norman'.

Although retired in the 1930s, 'Uncle Norman' was a tower of strength to us at Duxford in particular and 12 Group in general. Leigh-Mallory had served under him as Senior Air Staff Officer and the respect arising was mutual. I shall never forget one of our parties in the Mess when both 'LM' and 'Uncle Norman' were present. Someone produced some bagpipes, and in no time 'Uncle Norman's' Scottish blood took charge, and he did a sword dance on the table with a pair of crossed sticks instead of swords. 'LM' followed him, and although a Sassenach, he performed nearly as well as his old AOC. I think it must be the only time in history that two Air Vice-Marshals have done a sword dance at the same party!

'Uncle Norman' could fix anything, from supplies of sandbags for defence purposes and angle iron and broomsticks to make pikes from, to boiler-plate to act as armour plate behind the pilot's seat in our early unarmoured fighters or additional beer for the canteen. If we wanted any essential, and it could not be bought, he would requisition it. When it was vital, owing to bomb damage, that the Operations Room should be away from the aerodrome, he requisitioned Sawston Hall for us; we turned this fine old mansion into an up-to-date Operations Room, with sleeping and feeding accommodation on the premises for all our WAAF operations girls.

So many things were happening in those days that, dependant as I am solely on my memory; I hope I will be forgiven if I cannot mention actual dates, or if I record things in the wrong order.

DUXFORD 1940

About this time, just after the Fall of France, No 310 (Czech) Squadron was formed at Duxford. Most of the pilots reported in French uniform. After the invasion of Czechoslovakia they had joined the French Air Force. When they had no aircraft left they found their way to England by devious means. On arrival, however, they spoke little English, and had to be converted to our aircraft (Hawker Hurricanes in this case), so they were provided with an English squadron commander, flight commanders, flying instructor and an interpreter. Squadron Leader Douglas Blackwood was the English Squadron Commander, the Flight Commanders being Gordon Sinclair and Jefferies. The Czech CO was Squadron Leader Sasha Hess, who was to become a very good friend of mine. Sasha was quite famous in Air Force circles as, amongst other exploits, he had been the Czech Air Force Aerobatic Team Leader during peacetime. Much older than the rest at 45, he was a first class pilot and a dedicated fighter.

Our first problem was to overcome the language difficulties, so after much thought I rang Lance Sieveking at the BBC, with the result that, together with the Czech interpreter, I spent a day at Broadcasting House. There we recorded a series of orders, firstly in English followed by the Czech translation exactly as would be issued by the Sector Controller from 'scramble' (take-off) to 'pancake' (land) with every conceivable order in between. The BBC quickly sent us several copies of these records', and in a very short time the Czechs were conversant with the orders in English alone.

The Czechs, a handsome crowd, very quickly collected girl friends in the WAAF, and it was most amusing to guess from the accent they developed which WAAF taught English to which Czechs! Some developed Scottish, some Yorkshire, some Cockney accents; it gave us onlookers quite a lot of fun at the time.

No 310 (Czech) Squadron had a spare Hurricane, needless to say the oldest and slowest, which was always at my disposal, and as a result on the few occasions I could spare the time from my other duties as Section Commander and Sector Controller, I flew on operations with the Squadron as rear-end Charlie.

The Czechs were fine types and most of them had survived terrific hardships in their escape from Czechoslovakia after the German invasion. As one instance, Sasha Hess's wife and daughter had been taken to a concentration camp, and he had been informed that they were both dead. He could only hope that they had died quickly, but he vowed that he would never show mercy to any German, and would never take prisoners.

On the first occasion the Czechs got into action, early in the Battle of Britain, they made an excellent showing. I met them on their return to the aerodrome, and heard the following story from Sasha Hess:

Sasha disabled a Dornier over Epping Forest, and, with both engines stopped, it made a wheels-up landing in a field. He followed it down intending to ensure that no one got out alive. He saw three Germans climb out, who, when they realised that Sasha was diving on them, held up their hands. To quote his own words:

> I hesitate, then it was too late, so I go round again to make sure I kill them – they wave something white – again I did not shoot – then (disgustedly) – I think it is no damn use, I am become too bloody British!

I always consider that the Battle of Britain began just before the evacuation of Dunkirk, and more or less coincided with the over-running of Holland and Belgium. From Duxford our fighters were certainly heavily committed at that time. We made our first sortie over Holland with six Defiants of No 264 Squadron, led by Squadron Leader Philip Hunter, and six Spitfires as top cover, led by Rupert Leigh. Because of the long sea crossing they landed at Martlesham Heath the night before, re-fuelled and took off early the next morning. This was the first time the Boulton & Paul Defiant had been in action. It was an unusual fighter in that it was a two-seater with a four gun Frazer Nash Turret in the back seat, but no forward guns. At a distance it looked rather like a Hurricane, which misled the Germans on this first sortie, because, not knowing about the rear turret, the enemy fighters attacked from astern, being blown out of the sky by the terrific fire power they met. The Defiants shot down twice their own number on this occasion, and all our aircraft returned safely.

Unfortunately the press was informed of this victory and pictures of the Defiant were released and published in the national papers. This information obviously reached Germany very quickly, because when the operation was repeated two days later, the Germans attacked the Defiants head-on. Our casualties were very heavy and included Philip Hunter, the gallant Squadron Commander.

About this time one of our Spitfire squadrons was ordered to land at Manston and, after re-fuelling, patrol over Dunkirk. I flew down with them. When we arrived at Manston I was horrified to see about 50 or 60 aircraft all bunched together for re-fuelling in one corner of the aerodrome. One small bomb dropped on this bunch would have destroyed at least half a dozen aircraft. So, over the R/T, I ordered our Squadron to disperse at least 50 yards apart around the opposite side of the airfield after landing. When I climbed out of my Spitfire, I was greeted by an irate group captain who wanted to know why we had not taxied over to the already overcrowded re-fuelling area. Equally crossly I gave him the obvious answer, so the fuel tankers were driven round to our dispersed aircraft.

While our squadron was patrolling (unfortunately 'LM' had forbidden me to fly over France), to my amazement I saw my old Swordfish squadron, No 824 Fleet Air Arm Squadron, come in to land. I went over and greeted them and found that my old friend, Lieutenant Commander James Buckley, was leading them. They had been sent from Donnibristle in Scotland with orders to load up with 250 lb bombs, collect maps at Manston, and dive-bomb the advancing Germans behind Dunkirk. Out of nine aircraft only three returned from two sorties of this suicidal mission. James Buckley was shot down and made prisoner. Much later we heard that he had made a sensational escape, but was subsequently drowned in the Baltic.

From May to October 1940, we were all stretched to the limits of our endurance, but we were not in the least downhearted or pessimistic. As Station Commander I had to learn to snatch sleep in small doses. I had a camp bed in my office, and one in a cubbyhole in the Ops Room when, owing to the bombing, this was established at Sawston Hall. At all times I had to be within reach of a telephone. Early on we had a tannoy broadcasting system on the aerodrome, and this was in frequent use to call me to the nearest telephone. In that period I learnt to get the maximum benefit from even half-an-hour's sleep in a chair.

We had no airborne radar in 1940 at Duxford, and the searchlights depended upon sound locators. When we sent up Spitfires or Hurricanes at night they had to depend upon following the cone of searchlights to locate the enemy. On one of the first occasions when the enemy sent aircraft over East Anglia at night, John Petrie, a flight commander in 19 Squadron, was airborne, and the searchlights held the Heinkel in their beams long enough for John to shoot it down. Unfortunately, just after John had hit the enemy, the searchlight cone switched on his Spitfire. John, of course, was blinded in the glare, and the German rear-gunner fired a last burst at our aircraft before baling out. John's Spitfire burst into flames and he too baled out. I was an eyewitness to all of this, as it happened right over the aerodrome.

My immediate concern was for John Petrie, and after giving instructions for the civil police to round up the enemy, I sent search parties out. I next learned that John had been picked up suffering from nasty burns and taken to the nearest hospital. So giving orders that when captured the prisoners were to be placed in the Guardroom if unhurt, in the Station Sick-quarters under guard if injured, I set off in my car to see how John Petrie was fairing in hospital. Poor John, his face was badly burnt but his eyes had been saved by his goggles. I am glad to say that when Gillies or McIndoe, or both, made a magnificent plastic surgery job on his face, I next saw him as a highly decorated squadron leader in command of a Typhoon squadron in 1943, as fit and good looking as ever.

Dawn was just breaking as I returned to Duxford, and I was informed that the civil police had collected the prisoners and were bringing them in to our Guardroom. I left strict orders that there was to be no fraternising when the prisoners arrived – they were to be given a meal and cigarettes, and left in cells until collected by the security people. As I had not slept for 24 hours I then went to bed. At about 10.30 am, after a bath and shave, I asked about the prisoners and was told that there were two German NCOs in the cells whilst their officer had been taken over to the Officers' Mess.

I found the German pilot taking his ease in the Guest Room, cocktail in hand, chatting to Philip Hunter and several of our pilots. Our boys immediately stood up when I entered the room and said "Good morning, Sir", but the Hun, an arrogant young Nazi of about 20, remained lounging in his armchair and insolently eyed me up and down – but not for long. I got him to his feet smartly. Needless to say, I had him quickly transferred to the Guardroom cells. The boys thought me very hard-hearted and strict, but when the interrogation officers arrived they were very cross indeed, saying that "Chivalry is not understood by that type, they only regard it as a weakness". When I told the boys about how badly John Petrie had been burnt I think they understood my anger.

Soon after the fall of France, Leigh-Mallory rang me to say that No 242 (Canadian) Squadron were reporting to Coltishall and would be under the operational control of the Duxford Sector. He told me that the Squadron had had a tough time in France, and the groundcrews had been evacuated via Cherbourg, thanks to the resources of their Adjutant, Flight Lieutenant Peter MacDonald MP. Their own CO had left them to their own devices after the pilots had landed in England, and the squadron, led by Flying Officer Stan Turner (as he was then) had landed at Coltishall with nothing but the uniforms they were wearing. Tools, spare kit, and baggage – the lot had to be abandoned.

LM said, "I've got to find them a new Squadron Commander and he's got to be good, because these chaps are Canadians and have had a rough time – they are browned off with authority and need a good leader – any suggestions?"

At once I said "What about Douglas Bader?"

LM replied, "I thought you would say that. I think you are right."

So Douglas was promoted to Acting Squadron Leader and took command of 242 Squadron. The story of how, by sheer personal example, drive and leadership, he won the affection and loyalty of those tough Canadians, and built up their morale and esprit-de-corps until they established themselves as one of the best fighter squadrons in the Battle of Britain, has already been told in the book *Reach for the Sky* and shown in the film of the same name. I knew them all: Stan Turner, the chunky outspoken pipe-smoking Canadian, with whom I was later to serve at Tangmere and in Malta, Eric Ball, an Englishman from 19 Squadron, Powell-Sheddon with his attractive stutter that almost disappeared when he spoke on the R/T (we were also to meet again in Malta), Denis

Crowley-Milling, another old friend, Willie McKnight (later killed having been awarded the DFC and bar), Ben Brown and Cryderman, and the others, who all became an enthusiastic team led by their single minded and swashbuckling CO, Douglas Bader.

Douglas, of course, was very apt to cut corners, and ignore regulations or interpret them in his own way to get on with the war. On one occasion when he had offended against some rule, I was given orders from a higher authority to reprove him. He was ordered to report to my office, and when he stomped in and saluted with his usual cheerful grin he noticed that I was wearing my cap, and did not tell him to sit down, which indicated an official interview. Douglas stood to attention and with an impish grin said "Woody, you're not going to be rotten to me, are you?" What could I do but laugh, and then tell him to sit down? Needless to say the reproof was more or less passed to him as a joke – but the fact that it had been passed on proved quite effective.

As all aircraft were housed in widely dispersed shelter pens around the aerodrome we had a large hangar empty, so we built a full size stage for entertainment purposes. I discovered that Bill Whittle, a well-known cinema organist, was on the station as an aircrafthand, so we bought a Hammond electric organ out of PSI funds, and Bill Whittle and our amateur band played for regular dances. We bought roller skates – dozens of pairs – and the concrete floor proved admirable as a roller-skating rink. Thanks to the stage we attracted some excellent ENSA parties, with such famous artistes as Beatrice Lillie, Noel Coward and many others, giving of their best. These ENSA concerts were usually held on a Sunday nights when the artistes had their only night off from London shows.

One Sunday, after an excellent entertainment, we took the artistes back to the Officers' Mess for supper and refreshment, and many of the officers were there with their girlfriends. Two Czech pilots were night flying locally, using a glim-lamp flare path and a mobile Chance floodlight for landing. Although I had telephoned the Ops Room and been informed that there were no hostile plots on the board, we suddenly heard bombs explode on the aerodrome. First telling the WAAF officer to get the guests down to the shelters, I dashed to my car and drove to the aerodrome, where I found that a stick of bombs had been dropped on the flare path. The airman operating the Chance light had been wounded by a bomb fragment just before he switched off the motor, and four bomb craters were luckily on the centre line of the flare path 'T', and two of the glim-lamps had been extinguished.

In the meantime the two Czechs were still circling the aerodrome, with their navigation lights on, waiting to land, so having put the wounded man in the ambulance I dashed to the Watch Office, rang the Controller, told him to try and keep the Czechs airborne until we had fixed the flare path and Chance light, took one of the fire-tender crew with me to the Chance and started the motor, but just then the intruder dropped another stick of bombs, the last of which was close enough to splatter the airman and I with earth. As we picked ourselves up, I said very feelingly, "The bastard", to which the airman replied, with equal feeling, "You said it, Sir!"

Almost immediately the Czechs landed, luckily one on each side of the flare path, without navigation lights. It was miraculous that they did not collide. Having sent the Flying Control van to lead the Hurricanes back to their shelter pens, we extinguished the flare path and I tried to assess the damage. We had suffered several wounded, mostly Czechs at their dispersal, so when I had seen these casualties off to sick-quarters, I made a tour of the camp before sounding the 'All Clear', because I wanted to make sure that there were no further intruders about before allowing the off-duty personnel out of the dug-outs.

Luckily the living-quarters had escaped damage, and I found that Robbie, the WAAF officer, had shepherded all her flock, and the guests, down to the shelters, and the WAAFs were brewing tea there – but I couldn't find Robbie. At last I found her, sitting beside the bed of one of her girls. After rounding up her detachment to get them to safety, one was reported missing, so Robbie searched the quarters and found the girl shivering with fright, her head under the bedclothes. Robbie stayed with her as the girl was incapable of moving.

Everyone behaved extremely well on this occasion, particularly the women. The reason the raider was not reported until he dropped his bombs was that he probably sneaked in low across the coast, and so was not picked up by RDF. This attack by a single raider made us realise that wider dispersal was essential. The Operations Room, as the vital control centre of the Sector, was too vulnerable, situated as it was on the perimeter of the aerodrome. Thanks to 'Uncle Norman's' good offices Sawston Hall was requisitioned, and we went ahead with all speed to convert it to our requirements. By means of temporary partitions and facings of hardboard, the ancient panelling was preserved. Our radio personnel and Post & Telegraph Department rapidly organised the communications side and we obtained three Aga cookers to install in the enormous old kitchen. The WAAF Ops crew had their sleeping quarters on the upper floors, and when all was completed, we had a more efficient Operations Room several miles away from any obvious military target.

After the fall of France and the evacuation of our army from Dunkirk, we fully expected an attempted invasion. Apart from about a dozen rifles and the revolvers which had been issued to most of the pilots, we had no means of ground defence, so our inventive Engineering Officer made pikes out of broomsticks with sharpened angle iron wired on the end. The Transport Officer somehow 'won' an old heavy motor truck, and with boiler-plate, sandbags and a Lewis gun mounted on a Scarff ring, behind the cab, made a primitive armoured car – known as our 'Battle Wagon'!

After we had made these preparations, various army units were sent to take care of aerodrome defence, first a company of the London Scottish who were then relieved by a troop of the Queen's Bays who had recently (to their annoyance) exchanged their horses for Whippet tanks, and finally by a company of the Cameronians. The latter had been badly mauled in France and at Dunkirk, and were almost praying that the Hun would invade so that they could have their revenge.

The administrative and operational tasks and problems increased daily, and hampered as we were by a set of peacetime rules and regulations designed as they were to prevent petty pilfering, it is not surprising that everyone trying to do his job had to cut the 'red tape' in order to get on with the war. In this, Douglas Bader and I saw eye to eye, and I can claim that we backed each other up loyally in this matter of tape-cutting. 'LM', as my AOC, was always on my side too, which was very comforting. In those harassing times it was good to have a man like Jimmy Copley as Squadron Leader (Admin). An old RFC type, Jimmy had been Station Adjutant at Duxford in peacetime, and was promoted to Squadron Leader (Admin) when I assumed command. As the Battle of Britain developed, my operational responsibilities were so heavy that, had I not such an excellent administrative team working with me, on whom I could rely implicitly, we would have been in a sorry mess. The station strength had risen to 2,500, including 450 WAAF, ably commanded by little Flight Officer Margot Robinson (Robbie), who had already shown her qualities under the stress of bombing. The Operations team was grand too, and in that I include all the fighter controllers, Ops 'B' officers, signals, cyphers and teleprinter personnel of both sexes. All these had to learn their jobs from a small nucleus of RAF personnel, and they were good.

During that long summer of 1940, when even the weather seemed to favour the Germans, everyone on the station was working hard and, in spite of invasion threats, bad news of U-boat successes, and reverses in Crete and Greece, morale was high. Our casualties in the air were not light, but our victories outweighed them, and we knew that man for man, we were superior to the enemy. As we were fighting over our own country we had a certain advantage in that the loss of an aircraft did not necessarily mean the loss of a pilot too. On many occasions, hours and sometimes days after a pilot had failed to return with his squadron, he would walk into the Mess or be reported wounded and in hospital.

No 19 Squadron were re-armed with new Spitfires armed with two 20 mm cannons instead of the usual eight machine-guns. The Spitfire's wing section was so thin that the cannons had to be mounted on their side, meaning that, in spite of all our armourers' efforts, jamming was frequent. Almost every time they were used in combat the cannons had stoppages after a few rounds. On one occasion the squadron intercepted an enemy raid over Debden in ideal conditions, every aircraft had stoppages before half their ammunition had been expended, with the result that the enemy were barely damaged and we lost two aircraft.

This cannon failure was the culmination of a series of similar but not so serious ones, so I got on the telephone to 'LM' and urgently requested that the Squadron should have their eight-gun Spitfires back. The following afternoon the C-in-C, 'Stuffy' Dowding himself, landed at Duxford without warning. I greeted him and he gruffly said "I want to talk to 19 Squadron", so I drove him over to Fowlmere, the satellite airfield, where he met Sandy Lane, the Squadron Commander, and his pilots. Dowding listened to their complaints almost in silence, and then I drove him back to his aircraft (he was piloting himself) and as he climbed in he merely said, "You'll get your eight-gun Spitfires back". 'Stuffy' was a man of few words, he listened to all of us, asked a few pertinent questions, then made his decision. As a result of the C-in-C's visit, that same evening the instructors from the OTU at Hawarden flew their eight-gun Spitfires to Duxford and took back the cannon Spits.

The battle went on, with a steadily mounting credit score on our side, until that peak day of 15 September 1940, when the total enemy destroyed for the day by Fighter Command amounted to 185. Out of this number, the Duxford Wing, led by Douglas Bader, accounted for 52. After the war the Germans produced so-called official records to show that their number destroyed was only 79. I do not believe it. If their figure was correct, why did they stop? The fact remains that after 15 September they gave up large daylight raids, going over to night bombing. That, though, gave us a lot of headaches because airborne radar was only in the development stage, and we had pitifully few night-fighters. To combat this nocturnal menace we trained as many pilots as possible in night flying, but the Hurricanes and Spitfires were of very little use except in conditions of bright moonlight. They could only circle the target being bombed in the hope of seeing an enemy against the glare from the fires on the ground, and risks of collision were high. An intensive gun barrage seemed to be best at that time, but there were insufficient guns to protect all our major cities.

In October or November, President Benes of Czechoslovakia, with his Foreign Secretary, Jan Masaryck, and the Czech Air Force Chief, Air Vice-Marshal Janousek, came to the Station and inspected 310 Squadron. The President decorated a number of the Czech pilots, as well as Squadron Leader Douglas Blackwood and both English flight commanders, with the Czechoslovak War Cross (equivalent to our DFC). To my astonishment, President Benes pinned one to my chest too. I was also presented with the Czechoslovak silver Flying Sword, which is worn on the right breast pocket indicating that I was a fully qualified pilot in the Czech Air Force, and at the same time he produced authority from the Air Ministry for me to wear it. I was touched, because although Sasha Hess and his Squadron had known of the award for some time, they left it to their President to announce to me as a surprise.

Towards the end of 1940, Air Vice-Marshal Leigh-Mallory went to 11 Group and was relieved by Air Vice-Marshal Saul from 13 Group. Of course 'LM' was of such a stature that anyone would have found it difficult to step into his shoes. I will only say that where 'LM' led us, Saul thought it necessary to drive us. This did not make for happy relations between Group and Sector under the new regime.

I had grown more and more attached to our little WAAF officer, Margot Robinson, and we decided to get married. I knew that if it became known that we were married or even engaged, Margot would be posted away, so we married secretly in Cambridge on 9 January 1941, which was my birthday. The only people who knew were Air Vice-Marshal Norman McEwan (our best man), Marjorie Stiven (our Cypher Officer who was 'best girl') and Corporal Barratt, my RAF driver. We only had 24 hours leave and were back on duty the next day. The secret was well kept and we did not let anyone know until I was relieved in March.

Another, and more notable event, happened in January 1941: the King and Queen held an Investiture at Duxford. The King expressed the wish that it should be entirely a station affair, and that Group should not send any staff officers or inform the press. It had to be kept very secret because of the danger of a bombing raid if the news leaked to the Germans, who had already bombed Buckingham Palace when their Majesties were in residence the previous month. I was very nervous when the day arrived, but was relieved that the whole of East Anglia was blanketed with low cloud, with a base of 300 feet, although, of course, we kept a flight of Spitfires at instant readiness in case of emergency.

The King and Queen arrived by car, attended only by their Air Equerry, Wing Commander 'Mouse' Fielden, who eased my mind by detailing the seating arrangements for lunch. In addition to those from our own station there were about 70 other officers to be decorated, who had come for the investiture from neighbouring aerodromes. The dining room in the Officers' Mess wasn't large enough to accommodate all these guests as well as our own officers, so we had to arrange two sittings for lunch.

In spite of the King's wish, Air Vice-Marshal Saul arrived to greet him, and it was obvious that His Majesty was not pleased because after I introduced the AOC. I do not think His Majesty spoke to him again. For the investiture we had paraded all the Station personnel who were off duty in a large hangar. The airmen formed two sides of a hollow square, the WAAF detachment one side, and the officers to be decorated lined up across the top of the square. Before the ceremony, the King briefly inspected the male contingent while the Queen inspected the WAAF. The impression we were all left with was that they were not 'inspecting' in the military sense – they were presenting themselves for everyone (as Kipling says) 'For to behold and for to see'. Afterwards, Robbie told me that the Queen had a pleasant word to say to almost every one of her girls. Indeed, Her Majesty was so interested that the King had to send his Equerry to tell the Queen that the Investiture awaited.

After the ceremony we went over to the Mess for lunch. 'Mouse' Fielden had arranged the top table, with the King on my right, and the Queen on my left, with a Group Captain who had received the CBE on Her Majesty's left. I forget exactly who was on the King's right, but I do remember that AVM Saul was relegated to the extreme end of the top table. As the Queen was not attended by a Lady-in-Waiting, the senior WAAF officer was detailed for this necessary responsibility. It was a most memorable occasion; our Royal guests were quite charming to us all and made us feel at ease by making themselves at home. They were genuinely interested in everyone and everybody they saw.

After lunch, when we were having coffee in the ante-room, the Queen was taught the rudiments of 'shove ha-penny' by our young doctor. The King sat on the arm of a chair and watched. His Majesty idly picked up one of the 'ha-pennies', which were proper coins but smoothed off on one side – thank God, the tail side was defaced and not the King's head side! The King then said, "You know, a lot of the best games come from pubs!"

After coffee they had a friendly inspection of the station. We had some American Lend-Lease aircraft on the tarmac that the Air Fighting Development Unit (AFDU, a lodger unit on the Station) were putting through acceptance tests. The Queen asked if we had any photographs of them. I replied, "No, Ma-am, but we'll soon have them photographed".

Her Majesty replied, "That would be nice, the children would love to have copies". I then asked if I should send them to the Air Equerry, but the Queen said "No, address them to me, they'll get there quicker!"

We then drove their Majesties to see our Operations Room at Sawston Hall. The King was, of course, very interested in the fighter control side, but the Queen went off under Robbie's guidance and thoroughly explored all domestic arrangements, meeting a large number of the WAAF girls. While we were there a hostile plot crossed the coast. We scrambled two Spitfires immediately, which sighted the enemy over Norfolk before the Hun turned tail and escaped in cloud.

When in March 1941, it was decided that all Sector Stations should be commanded by a group captain, I was rather hurt to find that after commanding the Sector throughout the Battle of Britain, AVM Saul should decide to have me relieved by a groupie who commanded the AFDU. Doc Brown, our Station Medical Officer, who had been keeping his kindly professional eye on me, prescribed an immediate three weeks leave – I suppose I was rather tired.

When it was known that I was leaving Duxford the 'boys' hastily arranged a farewell party. On being told about this, I asked if I could bring my wife too. When I told them that Robbie and I had been married for three months they thought at first that I was pulling their legs. However, when AVM McEwan, who was of course invited to the party, told them that he had been at my wedding, I was believed, and the party became hilarious indeed. I felt more than a little sad, however, at leaving everyone after all we had been through together.

The next day, Margot and I set off on our deferred honeymoon, which we proposed to spend in Somerset. 'LM', who of course had heard that I had been superseded, and also been informed that I had a wife, telephoned and asked us to have lunch with him at 11 Group HQ, Uxbridge. He was, as usual, extremely charming to both of us, and wished us well. In parting, he merely said "Don't worry; I'll be seeing more of you, Woody".

We rusticated happily at a little farm near Waterrow in Somerset for a fortnight, when I was summoned to an Investiture at Buckingham Palace. Margot came with me, of course, and we met my sister, Dorothy, there. There were several of my Duxford friends there collecting 'gongs' too, so after the ceremony, which was most impressive, quite a gaggle of us, with our wives, sisters and girl-friends, went across to celebrate in the Ladies Dining Room of the RAF Club. At the Investiture, to my surprise and delight, I was told that I was posted to command Tangmere, with the rank of group captain. At the end of our leave, I drove Margot back to Duxford, where she resumed her duties as OC WAAF, then drove to Tangmere, pausing at 11 Group to thank 'LM' and receive his instructions.

At Tangmere, to my delight, I found Douglas Bader already there and in the properly established role of Wing Leader. With him were a lot of other old friends, with whom I was to begin another significant chapter of my life.

Woodhall's account is, to me, an absolute classic and gives us a great impression of life at Duxford during the Battle of Britain. His conclusions regarding the success of the 'Big Wing' theory, and the high number of claims by the squadrons involved, Bader's 242 in particular, have more recently been challenged by historians who have proved the inaccuracy involved (see *Bader's Duxford Fighters: The Big Wing Controversy* also by Dilip Sarkar). This is not the place to discuss those issues in detail, but it is worth clarifying that the German records were, in fact, correct (how could they not be, being as they were for the purposes of internal audit and not propaganda?). That we now know the 'Big Wing' not to have been as effective as its supporters believed is really irrelevant when it comes down to assessing the contribution made by Duxford and its personnel in 1940: the fact is that these men and women were there, in the front line, eager to have a crack at the enemy – and frequently did.

Contemporary photographs also provide us with a unique glimpse of the past. Many official photographs were taken at Duxford during the Battle of Britain, not least of Bader's Canadians and Blackwood's Czechs. Pilots of 19 and 616 Squadrons also provided the aircraft and personnel for a whole series of photographs illustrating the life and times of a fighter squadron (taken at Fowlmere). All of these photographs have been used on innumerable occasions to illustrate as many books and articles. Personal photography was of course forbidden on service installations, but nonetheless such unofficial pictures were taken. During the Battle of Britain, for example, 19 Squadron's Pilot Officer Peter Howard-Williams was a keen 'snapper', whose photographs were circulated around his fellow pilots and pasted into many a flying log book. In this book, therefore, I have concentrated on photographs such as those taken by 'Howard-Willy', but by necessity have also included some of the classic official photographs. This combination of pictures, preceded by 'Woody's' previously unpublished written account, will, I hope, breath life back into bygone Duxford; certainly the ghosts of many featured in the following photographs, I am sure, will never leave that hallowed place.

Abbreviations:			
	ACM	-	Air Chief Marshall
	AVM	-	Air Vice Marshall
	LAC	-	Leading Aircraftsman
	F/O	-	Flying Officer
	DFM	-	Distinguished Flying Medal
	S/L	-	Squadron Leader
	F/S	-	Flight Sargeant
	F/L	-	Flight Lieutenant
	P/O	-	Pilot Officer
	Sgt	-	Sergeant
	RFC	-	Royal Flying Corps
	WAAF	-	Women's Auxiliary Air Force
	AOC	-	Air Officer Commanding
	CO	-	Commanding Officer
	DFC	-	Distinguished Flying Cross
	NCO	-	Non Commissioned Officer
	WC	-	Wing Commander
	DSO	-	Distinguished Service Order
	IWM	-	Imperial War Museum

1. The first operational Spitfire, K9789, was delivered to No 19 Squadron at Duxford on 4 August 1938, by Supermarine Test Pilot Jeffrey Quill, a massively experienced pilot and an absolute gentleman, loved and respected by all. Sadly Jeffrey is now deceased but is pictured here in 1988, when the author had the privilege of meeting him at Duxford's celebrations to mark the fiftieth anniversary of that most historic occasion.

2. No 19 Squadron became famous as the RAF's first Spitfire squadron, the pilots of which are pictured here, outside the squadron's hangar at Duxford, in 1939.
From left to right, back row: Sgt Coleman, F/S Steere, Sgt Gunning, F/S Unwin, Sgt Potter.
Middle row: Unknown, P/Os Pace, Ball, Matheson, Petre, Llewellyn, Price & Marples, unknown.
Front row: P/Os Brinsden & Robinson, F/O Wythall, F/L Banham, S/L Cozens (CO), F/O Clouston, P/Os Coward & Sinclair.

3. No 19 Squadron's first Spitfires in May 1939, the 19 Squadron hangar, a recognisable landmark for any visitor to Duxford today, in the background. Note that the squadron's code letters are 'WZ'; they soon changed to 'QV' which remained constant throughout WW2.

4. Unofficial snapshot of an original 19 Squadron Spitfire Mk I. Note the fixed pitch Watts propeller, made of mahogany, the lack of an armoured windscreen, flat canopy sides, and the broom-handle like radio mast.

5. Another view of a Spitfire Mk I, showing the Perspex panel in the canopy, which could be punched out, and the early camouflage and marking scheme.

6. No 19 Squadron's first Spitfire flying accident: the pilot, P/O Gordon Sinclair (third from right in pre-war black flying suit), fortunately survived.

Left: 7. An excellent study of P/O 'Ace' Pace of No 19 Squadron, taken at Duxford during the winter of 1940. Of interest are the black pre-war flying overalls bearing the squadron crest.

Below: 8. P/O John Petre (left) & P/O Peter Howard-Williams, both of No 19 Squadron, pictured at Duxford that same winter. Petre scored one of the Spitfire's first nocturnal victories, but was himself shot down and badly burned in the process.

9. Petre's victim was this He 111 of 4/KG 4, which he shot down at Six Mile Bottom on 19 June 1940.

10. The Heinkel's crash site.

Above: 11. Incredibly the Heinkel's captain, Oblt Von Arnim, had known the wife of F/L Brian Lane, the commander of 19 Squadron's 'A' Flight, before the war on the continental motor racing circuit! Mrs Eileen Lane was visiting her husband at Duxford when recognised by Von Arnim, who was being held in the Officers' Mess. Mrs Lane was both a beautiful and intrepid young woman, who, like her fighter pilot husband, would sadly die prematurely. Eileen Lane is pictured here before the war in her Bugatti at Brooklands.

Left: 12. Brian Lane was an experienced pre-war fighter pilot who was posted to 19 Squadron as a flight commander on 11 September 1939. As a fighter pilot he was officially rated as 'exceptional', and so this proved to be during our 'Finest Hour'.

13. Brian and Eileen Lane pictured in February 1941, at the wedding of 19 Squadron's F/O Frank Brinsden. By that time Brian was a squadron leader, CO of 19 Squadron, and had been awarded the DFC.

14. F/O Frank Brinsden, a New Zealander (standing), F/O Matheson, an Australian, and F/L Lane, 1939.

15. Precious relic: Brian Lane's silver cigarette case, owned by the author and which he intends to one day donate to the IWM Duxford.

16. Early spring 1940: 19 Squadron's P/O Peter Howard-Williams (extreme left) & the CO, S/L Geoffrey Stephenson (who succeeded Henry Cozens in command, third right), with various non-flying personnel and two visiting French Air Force pilots. Stephenson would be shot down over Calais and captured on 26 May 1940, during the Squadron's first full formation combat.

17. Another early, unofficial, photograph, taken outside 19 Squadron's Watch Office in late 1938; from left, standing: P/Os 'Ace' Pace & Ian Robinson, F/L 'Wilf' Clouston, and F/Os John Banham & Eric Ball. Seated is F/O 'Tommy' Thomas, acting CO of 'A' Flight in F/L Pete Gordon's temporary absence.

18. A more formal but similarly unofficial photograph of 19 Squadron's 'B' flight pilots, amongst them F/S Harry Steere (extreme left, standing), P/O Gordon Sinclair (second right, standing), F/C 'Wilf' Clouston (seated, middle), and F/O James Coward (seated, extreme right).

19. Spring 1940: some of 'A' Flight's pilots: P/Os Lyne & Howard-Williams, F/O Matheson, Sgt Potter & P/O Watson. On the disastrous sortie during which S/L Stephenson was captured, Watson was killed in action.

20. An extremely rare air-to-air photograph snapped from the cockpit of P/O Michael Lyne's Spitfire in spring 1940: F/L Lane, Red One, leads, F/S Unwin flying as Red Two and Lyne himself, Red Three. Again the early colour scheme is shown.

Right: 21. P/O Michael Lyne, who was shot down and wounded over Dunkirk, consequently missing the Battle of Britain. He later flew Hurricanes on the perilous Merchant Ship Fighter Unit, survived the war and retired from the post war RAF as an air vice-marshal (sadly now deceased).

Below: 22. Another hitherto unpublished and informal snapshot of 19 Squadron at Duxford in September 1939. Those identified are: F/O Sinclair (second left), F/O Douglas Bader (smoking pipe, in civilian clothes), F/O Coward (third right), S/L Geoffrey Stephenson (fifth right), F/O Matheson (fourth right), F/O Clouston (first right), & F/O Brinsden (kneeling, first right). Coward would be shot down on 31 August 1940, losing his right foot.

23. Sgt Potter, F/O Matheson & P/O Watson. Potter pursued the enemy too close to the French coast on 15 September 1940, and was consequently shot down and captured.

24. Another remarkable snapshot taken of 19 Squadron during the 'Phoney War'. From left, front row: F/O Pace, P/O Brinsden, F/L Banham, F/L Clouston, unknown; middle row: F/O Petre, F/L Withall, P/Os Llewellyn & Ball; back row: unknown, P/O Watson, S/L Cozens, P/O Gordon, F/Os Sinclair & Coward, F/S Steere, Sgt Potter, F/S Unwin, final pair unknown.

25. Fred Roberts, from South Wales, was a young armourer on 19 Squadron before the war.

26. A photo frame, featuring a studio portrait of Fred Roberts, made from the Duralumin propeller tip of Spitfire K9809, in which P/O Trenchard perished in a night-flying accident in February 1940.

27 & 28. Having lost both legs in a blameworthy pre-war flying accident in 1931, F/O DRS Bader was thereafter unable to continue flying as a service pilot because King's Regulations did not cater for disabled pilots. Refusing to accept a ground role, Bader left the service but, when war with Germany became inevitable and pilots were badly needed, the Air Ministry agreed to reinstate him, providing the legless airman passed a flying test. Bader did so and was posted to 19 Squadron at Duxford, commanded by Geoffrey Stephenson, an old friend from Cranwell. Highly competitive, golf was a game Bader played on equal terms with the able bodied.

Right: 29. Ernie French was a member of 19 Squadron's ground crew and proudly recalls the days when he flew as Bader's passenger on 'jollies' in the Station's Miles Magister communications aircraft.

Below: 30. On 10 May 1940, the 'Phoney War' came to an abrupt and violent end when Hitler attacked the west. By 26 May the situation on the continent was so desperate that the decision was made for the British Expeditionary Force to retire on and be evacuated from Dunkirk. Spitfire squadrons gathered at fighter stations on or near the south coast to participate in Operation Dynamo, providing air cover. No 19 Squadron flew many patrols from Hornchurch, this snapshot being taken there and showing some of the squadron's armourers and assistants; from left: Bailey, Roberts, Stanley & Marshal.

DUXFORD 1940

31 & 32. On 26 May 1940, S/L Stephenson led 19 Squadron in a textbook Fighter Command attack on a gaggle of Stukas over Calais. Throttled right back, the Spitfires were bounced by Me 109s and suffered accordingly: Stephenson was shot down and captured and P/O Watson baled out but was never seen again. Further casualties followed that afternoon, a black day indeed for Duxford. These snapshots were taken by a German soldier and show Stephenson's Spitfire, N3200, on the beach at Coquelles, near Calais. Unusually the aircraft has no individual code letter.

33. During the late 1930s, 19 Squadron shared Duxford with No 66 Squadron, which became the RAF's second Spitfire squadron. This extremely rare air-to-air snapshot shows one of 66 Squadrons first Spitfire Mk Is, either 'LZ-P' or 'LZ-R'.

34. Members of 66 Squadron's groundcrew at Duxford. At centre is Jack Strachan, who served with 'Clickety-Click' from June 1939 – August 1940 (Via John Gillies).

DUXFORD 1940

Above: 35. The CO of 66 Squadron, S/L Fullergood (seated centre), with his officers at Duxford, probably in September 1939. Rear rank, from left: Rimmer, Smith, Oxspring, Paton, Campbell-Colquhoun, Grafstra (Canadian), Brown & Kennard. Seated, from left: Power (Australian), Browne, Jago, Fullergood, Heath, Thomas & Gillies. The photograph was taken outside the Watch Office, and, as anyone familiar with Duxford will know, the saplings are now large trees! (Via John Gillies).

Left: 36. F/L Ken Gillies of 66 Squadron, pictured at Duxford in 1939; sadly he would perish during the Battle of Britain. (John Gillies via Kennard).

Above: 37. Pilots of 66 Squadron at Readiness, Duxford. Taken by P/O Hugh Kennard, the snapshot shows the 'Ops' caravan at dispersal. From left: Peter Studd, Paton, Bobby Oxspring, unknown, Bill Smith, unknown (the latter being groundcrew). (John Gillies via Collingridge).

Right: 38. A 66 Squadron stalwart during the Battle of Britain was Rupert 'Lucky' Leigh, an Old Cranwellian and contemporary of Douglas Bader's. It was Leigh, in fact, who passed Bader fit to fly at the Central Flying School in 1939. Before the Battle of Britain 66 Squadron moved from Duxford, but was hotly engaged flying from 11 Group airfields during that epic aerial conflict.

DUXFORD 1940

Left: 39. HW 'Tubby' Mermagen. Another Duxford squadron during the early war period was No 222, operating the fighter version of the Bristol Blenheim. Commanded by another Old Cranwellian and former RAF aerobatic pilot, S/L HW 'Tubby' Mermagen, 222 was soon re-equipped with Spitfires. In February, 1940, Douglas Bader became one of Mermagen's flight commanders, and fought with the Squadron over Dunkirk.

Below: 40. No 222 Squadron also saw action over Dunkirk, F/L Douglas Bader being seen here at Manston with another soon-to-be fighter 'Ace', namely F/L Bob Stanford-Tuck of 92 Squadron (second right). The Spitfire is a 222 Squadron aircraft, probably Bader's, and of interest is the unusual dark coloured stripe painted beneath the nose.

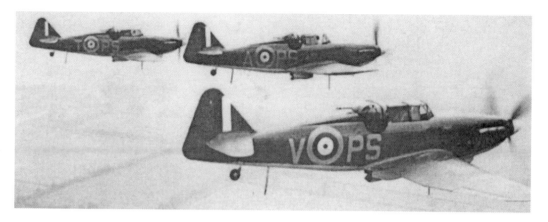

41. No 222 Squadron was replaced at Duxford by No 264, which operated the ill-fated Boulton-Paul Defiant. (All 264 Squadron photographs, courtesy Geoff Faulkner & the 264 Squadron Association).

42. No 264 Squadron's aircrew in May 1940, from left: LACs Cox, Wise, Fidler & Lille (all the LACs pictured were air gunners); P/O Webb, LAC Hayden, Sgt Lauder, P/Os Young & Stokes, Sgt Thorn, LAC Barker; Cpl Lippett, LACs King, Johnson & Fairbrother.

43. On 29 May 1940, 264 Squadron enjoyed success over the French coast when German fighters mistook them for Hurricanes, receiving a storm of lead in response from the Defiants' rear gunners. This photograph was taken between sorties at Manston on that particular day.

44. Pilots of 264 Squadron after their successful combat: the CO, S/L Hunter, is second from left, standing. Sadly he was killed in action soon afterwards, together with many of his aircrews, when the enemy realised their mistake and slaughtered the Defiants, which had no forward firing armament.

45. As 19 Squadron's CO was captured during the Dunkirk fighting, he was replaced by S/L Phillip 'Tommy' Pinkham AFC. Another Old Cranwellian and favourite of the Group Commander's, Pinkham had most recently taught Norwegians how to fly the Hurricane at St Athan, but had no combat experience.

46. In July 1940, 19 Squadron moved from the Duxford Sector Station to the nearby WW1 satellite airfield at Manor Farm, Fowlmere. Tents were erected and outbuildings improvised for accommodation until prefabricated Nissen huts were built. The idea was that if Duxford was bombed, with the sector's aircraft thus dispersed, damage would be minimised. Fowlmere was codenamed 'G1', and Duxford became 'G Sector'. This snapshot, by P/O Peter Howard-Williams, shows the Squadron's ops caravan and Intelligence Officer's bell tent.

Above: 47. Captioned 'Before the Blitz' in the logbook of P/O Arthur Vokes, this snapshot shows most of 19 Squadron's pilots at Fowlmere when the Battle of Britain started; left to right: F/L Lane, Sgts Potter & Jennings, P/O Aeberhardt, F/Ss Unwin & Steere, F/O Brinsden, F/L Lawson, P/Os Haines & Vokes, F/L Clouston & F/O Thomas. Interestingly, all of the pilots wear ties, as opposed to the stereotypical silk scarf. Several are wearing army battledress, and Clouston wears a much-prized German *schwimmveste*.

Left: 48. Amongst 19 Squadron's airframe riggers during the Battle of Britain was John Milne, who was allocated to work on P/O Howard-Williams' Spitfire, and also Brian Lane's aircraft.

49. John Milne's snapshot of the Airmen's Vegetable Garden at 'A' Flight's dispersal, on the west side of Duxford in spring 1940.

50. Lunch in the Officers' Mess at Fowlmere, a Nissen hut, and a far cry from the comparatively luxurious accommodation at nearby Duxford! Nearest to the camera are Frank Brinsden (left) and Brian Lane (right).

51. Cheers! 19 Squadron's officers enjoy a pint at Fowlmere: F/L Lawson at extreme left, F/L Lane at extreme right.

52. Another of 19 Squadron's successful pilots in 1940 was P/O Wallace 'Jock' Cunningham, pictured here (extreme right) at Fowlmere with F/O Brinsden (second right) and the Squadron Padre (extreme left). In the centre, Brian Lane, sporting the ribbon of his DFC, awarded for efforts during the Dunkirk fighting, and Sgt Bernard 'Jimmy' Jennings examine the former's 'Box Brownie' camera.

Right: 53. Brian Lane, camera in hand, although clearly unimpressed at being P/O Howard-Williams' subject!

Below: 54. P/O Howard-Williams, the snapper himself, photographed with his Spitfire and groundcrew at Fowlmere.

55. A more formal studio portrait of 'Howard-Willy', taken later in the war, by which time he had been awarded the DFC.

56. At Fowlmere, 19 Squadron re-equipped with the experimental Spitfire Mk IB, armed with two 20 mm cannons but no machine-guns. These aircraft proved unpopular due to stoppages and were eventually withdrawn. It has proved impossible to find a photograph of one of these aircraft, although this Mk IIB, snapped at Fowlmere in early 1941, is very similar. The pilot is Sgt Noel MacGregor, who joined the Squadron as a replacement in the autumn of 1940.

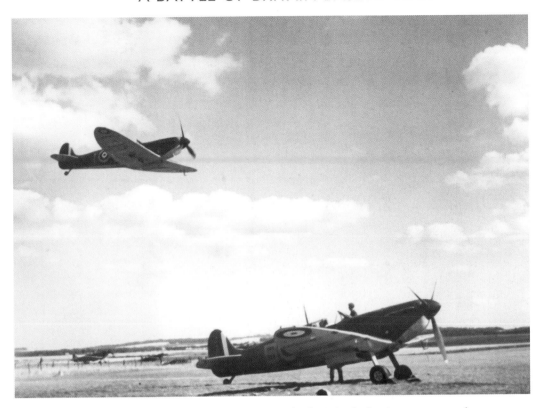

57. 19 Squadron Spitfires at Fowlmere during the Battle of Britain. Sgt Jennings passes over the photographer in 'QV-I', X4474.

58. A superb study of a 19 Squadron Spitfire being 'turned around' at Fowlmere after combat.

59. A Wellington snapped by John Milne over-flying Spitfires of 19 Squadron's 'A' Flight at Fowlmere during the Battle of Britain. Although of very poor quality, such snaps are unique.

60. A grass cutting tractor passes by two 'A' Flight Spitfires, 'QV-H' and 'QV-A', again snapped by John Milne. 'H' was the Spitfire flown by that incredibly tough fighter pilot from Yorkshire, George 'Grumpy' Unwin DFM.

61 & 62. Again, although of poor quality, these snapshots, taken by John Milne on rudimentary camera gear, show 19 Squadron Spitfires dispersed around Fowlmere early in 1941 – the scene unchanged from the summer of 1940.

DUXFORD 1940

Left: 63. Formal study of Birmingham's P/O Arthur Vokes, who flew Spitfires with 19 Squadron throughout the Battle of Britain and until his death in a flying accident the following year, by which time he was Acting CO.

Below: 64. Fortunately for Fighter Command, many trained pilots escaped when their countries were over-run by the Germans. Some, including Poles, Czechs, Belgians and French men, were posted as replacements to existing RAF squadrons, whilst others were formed into new squadrons of their fellow countrymen. Such was the case with 310 (Czech) Squadron, which formed at Duxford in July 1940 with Czech officers shadowing their British counterparts in command roles whilst the language difficulty and differences in operational procedures were overcome. S/L Douglas Blackwood (wearing peaked cap) became the British CO, shadowed by S/L Sasha Hess, and F/L Gordon Sinclair (in forage cap) became a flight commander.

65. From left: F/L Sinclair, P/O Janough, F/O Chesney (Adjutant), P/Os Puda & Kaucky and F/L Jeffries, all of 310 Squadron.

66. Another staged press photograph of 310 Squadron, F/L Jeffries kneeling, third right, and F/O Boulton seventh from right.

67. An informal snapshot of 310 Squadron's Czech pilots.

68. From left: F/O Boulton, F/Ls Jeffries & Sinclair. Sadly Boulton was killed when he and Sinclair collided in mid-air over London during a combat on 15 September 1940.

69. Unofficial snapshot by Orderly Clerk Bill Kirk of a 310 Squadron Hurricane and airman.

70. An excited S/L Sasha Hess recounts how he shot down two 'Bloddy Germans' on 31 August 1940. Behind is his personal Hurricane, 'NN-A', R4085.

71 & 72. Two official photographs of 310 Squadron's Sgt Furst.

73 & 74. Czech 'plumbers' arming Sgt Furst's Hurricane.

75. A 310 Squadron Hurricane has its guns harmonised at Duxford during the Battle of Britain.

76. No 310 Squadron Hurricanes low over Duxford – the leading aircraft flying the tight 'vic' advocated by Fighter Command's tacticians, but which was to prove useless in combat.

77 & 78. Snaps from the album of Sergeant Bill Kirk (extreme right in 77 & extreme left in 78), an Orderly Clerk on 310 Squadron.

79. S/L Douglas Bader (seated, front centre) with his Canadian pilots of 242 Squadron. Although based at Coltishall, from September 1940, onwards, 242 operated from Duxford.

80. 242 Squadron had taken a beating in France; morale being in poor shape when Bader took command. That he restored the situation is evident from these smiling faces, indicating the lighter side of squadron life, Bader himself appearing to play Napoleon in this charade.

Above: 81. More 242 Squadron tomfoolery!

Right: 82. F/L Eric Ball, S/L Bader & the Canadian F/O JB Latta at Duxford.

83. For all his faults, Bader's enthusiasm and energy was infectious: he was an inspired choice of leader for the disillusioned Canadians.

84. Bader's pilots of 242 Squadron outside the Officers' Mess at Duxford.

85. Naturally Bader, the legless fighter 'Ace', became a magnet for wartime propaganda, and after the war, became a household name through Paul Brickhill's best selling book *Reach for the Sky* and Danny Angels movie of the same name. Consequently, many people, I am sure, still believe that the Battle of Britain was won single-handedly by Bader and 242 Squadron!

86 & 87. Situated in 12 Group, the role of Duxford's squadrons was to defend the industrial Midlands and the North, and to provide cover for 11 Group's airfields whilst AVM Park's fighters were engaged. These tactics were a fundamental part of ACM Sir Hugh Dowding's System of Air Defence, but Bader, frustrated at having to play a secondary role whilst the battle raged over southern England, formulated his controversial 'Big Wing' tactics. Bader, a junior acting squadron leader, believed that fighters should be deployed en masse, rather than in the penny-packet formations advocated by his commander-in-chief, who, outside Germany, knew more about fighter warfare than any man alive. However, Bader found support in his group commander, AVM Leigh-Mallory, who also resented playing a lesser role and who gave permission for 242, 310 and 19 Squadrons to fly together. These two photographs perfectly illustrate the boredom and dissatisfaction felt by Bader and his pilots.

Right: 88. In addition to the AOC 12 group commander, AVM Leigh-Mallory (centre), Bader's theory also won support from Duxford's station commander and 'Boss Controller', Grp Capt EB 'Woody' Woodhall (left). The so-called 'Duxford Wing' first flew on 7 September 1940, although the sortie was not a resounding success. Nonetheless, Leigh-Mallory immediately ordered that 302 and 611 Squadrons join the party.

Below: 89. Bader's adjutant, F/L Peter MacDonald, was an MP who had Churchill's ear, so the 'Big Wing' theory won support in very high places. Here Bader is pictured at Duxford with the air minister, Sir Archibald Sinclair.

90. AVM Sir Trafford Leigh-Mallory was determined that not all the glory should go to No 11 Group, and saw the 'Big Wing' as a means to this end. This man, who commanded a fighter group during our 'Finest Hour', however, had no personal experience of fighter combat or command.

91. HM King George VI with the AOC-in-C of Fighter Command, ACM Sir Hugh Dowding. Although known as 'Stuffy', Dowding, a Great War fighter pilot and squadron commander, cared deeply about his 'chicks', as demonstrated by him personally flying to Duxford and hearing first hand 19 Squadron's complaints about the Spitfire Mk IB.

Above: 92. AVM Keith Park, a tough New Zealander and Great War fighter pilot, fully supported Dowding's tactics, but too late saw the support gathering against them, engineered by Leigh-Mallory. Nonetheless, it was Dowding and Park who won the Battle of Britain, the record confirming that their tactics of conserving strength were right. Although the 'Big Wing' claimed great numbers of enemy aircraft destroyed, the record proves that this was not the case, the claims being generated purely by confusion given the numbers of fighters engaged.

Right: 93. When the situation became critical, Fighter Command received an influx of volunteers from other commands and even services. Sub-Lts Cork and Gardner of the Fleet Air Arm, for example, were popular members of 242 Squadron, Bader deciding that they were both 'good types'.

Left: 94. Very few airmen are mentioned by name in the film '*Reach for the Sky*', Woodhall, the Canadian Stan Turner and young Denis Crowley-Milling being notable exceptions. Known universally as 'Crow' or 'DCM', Crowley-Milling was an Old Malvernian and a VR pilot. Impressionable and enthusiastic, Crow flew Hurricanes in 242 Squadron and worshipped his swashbuckling CO. After Bader's death in 1982, Crow became a founder member of the Douglas Bader Foundation, a charity offering support to the amputee disabled, in memory of Sir Douglas. Crow retired from the post war RAF as an Air Marshal and died in 1996.

Below: 95. Hurricane P3715, 'LE-H', of 242 Squadron, in which Crow was shot up on 7 September 1940. Caught on the climb by Me 109s, Bader later wrote, 'It was windy work, make no mistake'.

96 & 97. Crow displays the armoured windscreen, which saved his life, from P3715.

98. Crow, complete with roll neck sweater, Mae West, black pre-war flying suit and Hawker Hurricane.

99. One of Bader's Canadians, P/O John Benzie, was also shot down on 7 September 1940: the twenty-five year old remains missing to this day.

Right: 100. The Poles of 302 Squadron also flew from Duxford as part of the 'Big Wing', this being Sgt Antoni Markiewicz who recalls that, "If ever we missed the Germans, Bader would be very displeased and let us know in very simple language!"

Below: 101. The Spitfires of Digby's Auxiliary 611 Squadron also flew with the 'Big Wing', operating from Fowlmere with 19 Squadron. The CO, S/L James McComb, is pictured above (fourth from right) with his pilots just after Dunkirk.

102. No 611 Squadron's place in the line was replaced by 616 Squadron, which had made progress in re-building after being virtually annihilated flying from Kenley in August 1940. At this time, due to an administrative error, both 92 and 616 Squadrons shared the code letters 'QJ'. Genuine photographs of the latter's aircraft are rare, but this photograph does indeed show 616 Squadron Spitfires at Fowlmere in September 1940.

103. One young 616 Squadron pilot shot down and wounded whilst flying out of Kenley was P/O Hugh 'Cocky' Dundas. Returning to operations with the Duxford Wing, Dundas found the security of numbers comforting and Bader inspirational. Like Crow, he would remain a lifelong friend of the legless airman, and was also a founder member of the Douglas Bader Foundation. Again, this is a very rare photograph of a 616 Squadron Spitfire during the Battle of Britain.

Above: 104. After the Battle of Britain, 242 Squadron resumed operations from Coltishall, largely flying convoy patrols. In March 1941, Douglas Bader became Wing Commander (Flying) at Tangmere, near Chichester, leading the wing from the head of 616 Squadron. On 9 August 1941, Bader was brought down over France and captured. In 1995, the author's research confirmed that the Tangmere Wing Leader had actually been the victim of 'friendly fire', the pilot responsible being 616 Squadron Battle of Britain veteran F/O Lionel 'Buck' Casson, pictured in the cricket sweater. The other pilots are F/L Colin MacFie, S/L Ken Holden and F/O Hugh Dundas; all three flew on operations with the Duxford Wing in 1940.

Right: 105. The role of women in the Battle of Britain must not be forgotten. Jill 'Half Pint' Pepper was a plotter in Duxford's Sector Operations Room.

Above: 106. In 1997, Jill returned to Duxford, attending the launch of the author's *Bader's Duxford Fighters: The Big Wing Controversy* to visit her old place of work from 1940, when she was aged 19.

Left: 107. Another plotter on Ops 'B' was Margaret Balfour.

108. P/O 'Teddy' Morton, an Ops 'B' controller, who worked closely with Grp Capt Woodhall in the Sector Operations Room.

109. Margaret Balfour and 'Teddy' Morton reunited at a Battle of Britain symposium organised by the author at Worcester in 1998; sadly both are now deceased.

110. On 21 September 1940, the press descended upon Fowlmere and took numerous photographs to illustrate life on a typical Spitfire squadron. The photographers' subjects were the pilots and aircraft of both 19 and 616 Squadrons. In this photograph a pilot of 19 Squadron prepares for take off.

111. Sgt Jennings about to take up 'QV-I', X4474, and 'beat up' the airfield for the photographers' benefit.

112. Sgt Jennings about to become unstuck from terra firma.

113. Sgt Jennings and Spitfire in perfect harmony.

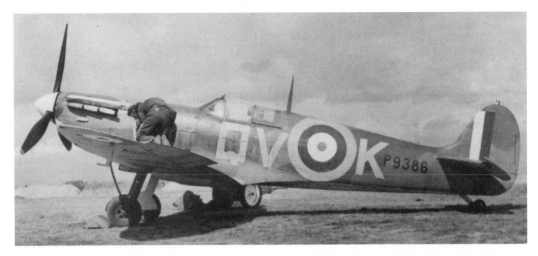

114. On 5 September 1940, S/L Pinkham was killed in his first combat, his successor being Brian Lane. This is S/L Lane's Spitfire, 'QV-K', P9386, one of the machine-gun armed Mk IAs that replaced the unreliable Mk IBs, in which 19 Squadron had lost all confidence. This Spitfire eventually perished with its pilot in a flying accident in Scotland.

115. S/L Lane pictured at Fowlmere by a press photographer. Interestingly, some of 19 Squadron's pilots were wearing battledress, which had yet to be widely issued at that time.

116. S/L Lane, centre, debriefs after a sortie with F/L Walter 'Farmer' Lawson DFC (left) and F/S George Unwin DFM. The strain on the young CO's face is all too evident.

117. Lane and Lawson are joined by the Sgt Lloyd and the Squadron Intelligence Officer, F/O Crastor. In the background is Unwin's Spitfire.

118. P/O Wallace 'Jock' Cunningham, who received a DFC for his efforts during the Battle of Britain, but who fell victim to anti-aircraft fire over Holland and was captured the following year.

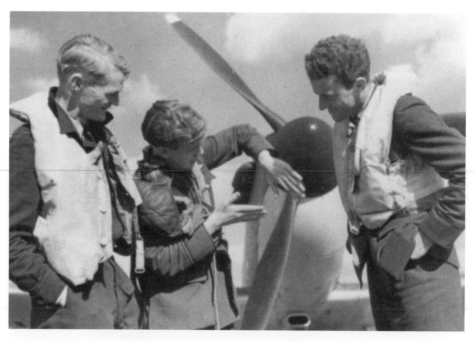

119. No 19 Squadron's P/O Leonard Haines 'shoots a line' to F/O Frank Brinsden (left) and P/O 'Uncle Sam' Leckrone, an American volunteer serving with 616 Squadron.

120. P/O Frantizek Dolezal, a Czech serving with 19 Squadron.

121. At 'Readiness': from left (with pipe): F/L Colin MacFie (616), S/L Billy Burton (CO, 616), S/L Brian Lane DFC (CO, 19), F/O Hugh 'Cocky' Dundas (616), P/O Richard Jones (19), remainder unknown but presumed 616.

122. F/S George Unwin DFM, F/L Walter Lawson DFC and Sgt David Lloyd walking in after a sortie, Unwin and Lawson clutching combat report forms.

123. Left to right: unknown, Sub-Lt Blake (19, obscured), unknown, S/L Lane (19), P/O Dundas (616, head only visible), unknown, F/S Steere DFM, F/L Lawson DFC (19, kneeling), P/O Hradil (Czech, 19), Sgt Lloyd (19), next two unknown, Sgt Jennings and F/S Unwin's beloved dog, 'Flash'.

124. Left to right: Sgt Lloyd (19), F/S Unwin DFM (19), unknown, P/O Dundas (616), F/S Steere DFM (19), S/L Lane (19).

125. Briefing, from left: F/O Brinsden (19), Sgt Charnock (19), P/O Haines (19), S/L Lane DFC (19), P/O Leckrone (616), Sgt Cox (19), F/S Unwin (19), P/O Jones (19), Sgt Jennings (19), unknown, F/L MacFie (obscured, wearing scarf, 616), F/L Holden (616).

126. P/O Richard Leoline Jones, 19 Squadron.

127. F/S George 'Grumpy' Unwin DFM & bar with 'Flash'. A miner's son from Yorkshire, but with a grammar school education, George made the quantum leap from 'Halton Brat' to fighter pilot. The first NCO pilot to ever fly a Spitfire, he was amongst Fighter Command's most aggressive and successful fighter pilots in 1940. Unwin later saw post war action during the Malayan Emergency, commanding a Brigand squadron and for which he received the DSO.

128. W/C Unwin pictured at his Wimbourne home shortly before his death, aged 92, in 2006. 'Grumpy' was both a friend of an inspiration to the author for many years, and the author was privileged to speak at the W/C's funeral.

129. A final, iconic, image from the photographs of 21 September: in a posed shot, armourer Fred Roberts attends to the ammo tanks whilst a rigger assists Sgt Jennings from the cockpit.

130. In 1993, the author reunited Fred Roberts and W/C Jennings at a book signing; sadly the latter is now deceased.

131. In 2006, the author published Fred Roberts memoir, 'From Duxford to Karachi. Fred remains extremely proud of his Battle of Britain service with 19 Squadron, during which he survived being bombed at Fowlmere, and worked on the Spitfires of S/L Lane and F/S Unwin. Fred's grandson has recently been commissioned into the RAF.

Right: 132. Fighter pilot: 19 Squadron's F/O Thomas. The leather flying helmet is painted yellow, in an attempt to increase visibility if shot down into the sea.

Below: 133. The Czech Sgt Plzak at Fowlmere in September, posing with the Spitfire made famous on 21 September, 1940, by Sgt Jennings.

134 & 135. The Czech P/O, 'Dolly' Dolezal, with a Spitfire Mk IIA at Fowlmere in September 1940. Note the Rotol Constant Speed propeller, a huge improvement on the original fixed pitch airscrews.

136 & 137. The Czech P/O Hradil poses with the same aircraft. Shot down over Southend on 5 November, 1940, he remains missing in action.

138. The 'Three Musketeers': Czech pilots Dolezal, Plzak and Hradil. The transport belonged to George Unwin, whose dog, 'Flash', was the usual sidecar passenger!

139, 140 & 141. Sub-Lt Arthur Giles Blake, inevitably known as the 'Admiral', of the FAA who flew Spitfires with 19 Squadron; sadly he was not to survive the Battle of Britain.

142. Air Commodore James Coward, an Australian, was a F/O with 19 Squadron during our Finest Hour. Shot down defending Duxford on 31 August 1940, he baled out only to realise that he was bleeding to death, his left foot hanging on by the skin. Using his helmet's radio lead to tie a tourniquet, Coward survived.

143. The Spitfire in which F/O Coward was shot down, X4231, was an important one given that it was the first with a wing including both cannon and machine-gun armament. In more recent years the crash site has been excavated, aviation archaeologist Richard Payne recovering one of those historic 20 mm Hispano-Suiza cannons. (Roger Mills).

Right: 144. No 19 Squadron's nineteen-year-old P/O Ray Aeberhardt's luck ran out on 31 August 1940. Returning to Fowlmere after a combat, his flaps failed, the Spitfire crashing and bursting into flame.

Below: 145. Before the Battle of Britain, Sgt David Cox became 19 Squadron's first pilot from the VR stable. A successful fighter pilot during 1940, 'Coxy' also survived being shot down himself. He later fought with distinction over North Africa, became an 'Ace' and received the DFC.

146. The 'impish' Wing Commander DGSR Cox DFC, pictured at home by the author in 1989; sadly this tremendously enthusiastic and fine gentleman has since died.

147. Many other VR pilots would follow David Cox into 19, and, indeed, many other fighter squadrons. Amongst the men was P/O Richard L Jones. Having already flown Spitfires with 64 Squadron in 11 Group, Richard was posted to 19 in 12 Group in September 1940.

Right: 148. During the Battle of Britain, P/O Jones married his sweetheart, Elizabeth, who was 19. Pictured here on their wedding day, at the time of writing the happy couple have now been married for over 68 years!

Below: 149. Richard L Jones has been a great supporter of the author's work in commemorating the Battle of Britain, and is pictured here discussing his experiences at the author's old school at Sibford Ferris, Oxon.

150. Towards the end of the Battle of Britain, another VR replacement arrived at 19 Squadron, namely Sgt Ken Wilkinson, from Cheltenham.

151. Ken Wilkinson, pictured more recently, at one of the author's many book signings.

Above: 152. One professional airman serving on 19 Squadron during the Battle of Britain was P/O Eric Burgoyne, a short service commission pilot. Here he poses with P9391, having been hit by 20 mm cannon shells in combat with Me 109s over the Thames Estuary. The date was 5 September, 1940, and S/L Pinkham AFC was killed in the same action. Of interest is the unusual location, size and style of the aircraft's serial number. Sadly Burgoyne was not to survive the Battle of Britain.

Right: 153. F/O Alan Haines DFC, another professional airman, was one of 19 Squadron's 'Aces', but was killed in a flying accident whilst serving as an instructor after the Battle of Britain.

Left: 154. Amongst F/O Haines' victims was an Me 109 of I/JG 54, which crashed at Hardy Street, Maidstone, on 5 September 1940; fortunately the occupants were not at home!

Below: 155. Amongst 19 Squadron's pre-war pilots was Frank Brinsden, pictured here at Fowlmere. A New Zealander, Frank later flew Mosquitoes but was captured on the famous Peenemunde raid when one of his propellers touched the north sea. Both pilot and navigator survived and took to their dinghy, before being captured by the Germans. W/C Brinsden visited the author in 1990, but sadly died soon afterwards.

156. P/Os Wallace 'Jock' Cunningham DFC and Eric Burgoyne at Fowlmere.

157. P/O Cunningham is joined 'at Readiness' by Sub-Lt Blake and F/O Brinsden.

158. P/O Dolezal joins the trio; he survived the war, only to lose his life shortly afterwards in a flying accident back in his native homeland.

159. P/O Richard Jones reads a letter whilst awaiting the call to 'scramble', with the Squadron Intelligence Officer, F/O Crastor.

160. Having survived being shot up on 5 September P/O Burgoyne, pictured here with P/O Parrott, was killed in action on 27 September 1940.

161. Another 'Howard-Willy' snap: S/L Lane's Spitfire Mk IIA in October 1940. Note the non-regulation and fared in mirrors. When asked to remove them by a wingless air commodore, Brian allegedly replied "Well, you fly the bloody thing, then!"

162. A favourite amongst the 'Few': Sgt Bernard 'Jimmy' Jennings DFM. In November 1940, S/L Lane was accidentally shot down by a Hurricane but fortunately forced-landed at Eastchurch. In his logbook, the 19 Squadron CO wrote 'Jennings followed me down, damn good of him'. Another regular guest at the author's many book signings, although Jimmy died some years ago, his memory, and sense of humour, lives on. Amongst the many stories he delighted in telling was the one that 19 Squadron turned away P/O Johnnie Johnson, who reported as a replacement pilot on 5 September 1940, 'because we were too busy to teach him how to fly properly!'

163. As we all know, Johnnie went on to become the RAF's top scoring fighter pilot and, in this author's opinion, the best Wing Leader of WW2. P/O Johnson is pictured here at Kirton during the winter of 1940, whilst serving with 616 Squadron, which was not too busy to teach him how to 'fly properly'!

Right: 164. Sgt Jack Potter of 19 Squadron, pictured at Duxford in 1940. Like Jennings, he too was a regular NCO. Having pursued the enemy too close to France, Potter was shot down and captured. He died in the 1990s.

Below: 165. During the Battle of Britain, David Fulford was a Sgt Pilot with 19 Squadron. Commissioned shortly afterwards, he subsequently flew Spitfires with 118 Squadron but was sadly killed in action before the war's end.

166. Sadly, many of the 'Few' who survived shot and shell in 1940 would not see out the war. On D-Day plus 3, Harry Steere, George Unwin's running mate and fellow F/S in 19 Squadron, was killed flying a Mosquito over Normandy.

167. At Fowlmere the Duxford Sector's Spitfire pilots managed to avail themselves of shooting both clays and pigeons. Shooting such moving aerial targets was great practice for their grim trade. Here 'Farmer' Lawson takes aim at a clay.

168. Oops! 'Farmer' Lawson recovers a homing pigeon, shot in error! P/O Jock Cunningham, with eye patch, and Sgt Cox look on.

169. Lawson was a pre-war airman and received the DFC for his Battle of Britain efforts. In 1941, he succeeded Brian Lane in command of 19 Squadron, but was killed in action soon afterwards when shot down by 109s into the North Sea; he remains missing in action. This was an absolutely futile operation, escorting light bombers attacking shipping at Rotterdam, which also saw F/L 'Jock' Cunningham DFC brought down by ground fire and captured.

Above: 170. P9546 had been damaged by a bullet in the main spar during the Battle of Britain, and eventually broke up in mid-air whilst on a training flight during 1941. This is the crash site at Dymock, Gloucestershire.

Left: 171. Sadly, within this historic Battle of Britain Spitfire, which was actually the regular mount of F/S Unwin and in which he too scored victories, perished the Canadian pilot, nineteen-year-old, Sgt George Alvin Davies.

172. A snap from David Cox's album of 19 Squadron over Duxford in September, 1940, although the bare trees suggest that this could be later.

173. From Richard Jones's album comes this equally rare snapshot captioned 'During an air raid', September 1940, Fowlmere; from left: unknown groundcrew F/S in 'battle bowler', P/O Parrott, Sgt Lloyd & P/O Hradil.

Left: 174. At 35, Harry Walpole Charnock was somewhat old to be a fighter pilot in 1940. He was actually an Old Cranwellian who had flown with Nos 1 and 32 Squadrons before the war, until being cashiered for a low flying offence in 1930. When war broke out he re-joined the RAF, flying Spitfires with 64 Squadron before being posted to 19 Squadron as a replacement in October 1940. During that tour he destroyed three German fighters, earning a DFM, and later became most successful over North Africa. He was re-commissioned in 1943, and received the DFC. Charnock ended the war a F/L, left the RAF in 1945, and died in 1974.

Below: 175. Clearly flying and fighting the enemy was insufficient excitement for the Czechs, seen here outside the pilots' hut teasing 'Flash'!

176. Today, all is quiet at Fowlmere, the Spitfires gone long ago. (Andrew Long).

177. After the Battle of Britain came the accolades and just awards for gallant service. Amongst the first of the VIP visitors was the President of Czechoslovakia in exile, President Benes. Here Grp Capt Woodhall, in greatcoat, awaits the President at Duxford with British and Czech pilots of 310 Squadron. Behind Woodhall, left to right, are S/L Blackwood with his flight commanders, F/L Jeffries and Sinclair; the foremost officer is S/L Sasha Hess, the Czech CO.

178. President Benes confers a Czech gallantry decoration upon S/L Blackwood, whilst Jeffries maintains strictly eyes front.

179. The President addresses his fellow Czech patriots.

180. No 310 Squadron groundcrew prepares to march past.

181. Duxford personnel march past in honour of President Benes.

182. Next came a Royal visit, when the King and Queen of England attended Duxford for an Investiture. Here 19 Squadron's Adjutant, F/O Budd, awaits their Majesties with P/Os Cunningham DFC and Vokes.

183. The King presents the DFC to 310 Squadron's F/L Jeffries.

184. The Czech CO of 310 Squadron, S/L Sasha Hess, proudly receives his DFC from King George VI.

185. Czech pilots on parade for the Royal visit.

Above: 186. Congratulations! S/L Hess shakes hands with F/L Jeffries. Next to Jeffries are 19 Squadron's F/O Haines and F/L Lawson, both of whom also received DFCs. Any visitor to the IWM Duxford today could easily identify this very spot, given the prominent landmark at to the left.

Left: 187. The Queen became immediately popular with the pilots when Her Majesty played 'Shove ha'penny' in the pilots' hut! Here F/L Lawson is photographed for posterity at that very table. Many years later, The Queen Mother, as Her Majesty became, would later become Patron of the Battle of Britain Fighter Association.

188. There was still much fighting left to do, however, even though the Battle of Britain was officially over on 31 October 1940. Like every other fighter squadron, 19 Squadron reflected a line up of old and familiar faces alongside new boys; from left to right, standing: Sgt Charnock, F/O Brinsden, P/O Hradil, Sgts Fulford, Lloyd & Boswell; from left, kneeling: P/O Parrott, P/O Dolezal, F/L Lawson DFC, F/S Unwin DFM, Sgt MacGregor.

189 (previous page) – 191. The Spitfire Mk IAs of the Battle of Britain were generally all replaced by now with the improved Mk IIA. These remarkable air-to-air pictures show Mk IIAs of 19 Squadron's 'A' Flight over Cambridgeshire just after the Battle of Britain, and were snapped from the cockpit of P/O Scott's Spitfire. Inevitably S/L Lane DFC leads, the other pilots being P/Os Stevens & Vokes with F/Ls Cunningham DFC & Lawson DFC.

192. Fighter Pilot: epitomising a whole generation of fighter pilots who went to war from Duxford in 1940, F/L Colin MacFie of 616 Squadron.

193. Grp Capt AB 'Woody' Woodhall, Duxford's popular station commander and sector controller.

Above: 194. Early in 1941, the popular S/L Brian Lane DFC was posted on a staff appointment, and succeeded in command by 'Farmer' Lawson DFC. This snapshot was taken by P/O Michael Lyne just before the hand over ceremony, and is remarkable given that although of poor quality, the original is in colour. Those identified are the Adjutant, F/O Budd at extreme left, Lawson fourth from left, S/L Lane sixth from left, and P/O Vokes, extreme right.

Left: 195. Sent to the Middle East, the climate disagreed with S/L Lane, who returned to the UK for a refresher course on Spitfires at Rednal in Shropshire. Sadly, whilst flying as supernumerary with 167 Squadron, S/L Lane was shot down by an FW 190 over the North Sea on 13 December 1942. His body was never found, and this outstanding young man is remembered on the Runnymede Memorial, together with so many of those who flew and fought in 1940.

Right: 196. Today the survivors get fewer as time marches ever on, but all recall vividly their days at Duxford during the Battle of Britain and insist that they were the most exciting days of their lives. Here are pictured three proud 19 Squadron groundcrew veterans, namely, from left, John Milne, Fred Roberts & Ernie French, all of whom are mentioned elsewhere in this book.

Below: 197. Over the last eighteen years, the author's book signings and other Battle of Britain related events have given survivors an opportunity to become re-acquainted and re-live old times; from left: Fred Roberts (19 Squadron), Bob Morris (who served as a Fitter IIE on 66 Squadron at Duxford), and Bill Kirk (310 Squadron).

198. Many veterans have welcomed the opportunity to recount their experiences, amongst them Richard L Jones, posing here at home with a photograph taken of himself at Fowlmere during 1940, which he bought at a car boot sale!

199. The author's book signings have also provided an opportunity for the general public to meet personalities from the pages of history; he is pictured here with Lady Bader and Richard L Jones in 1998. All of the other pilots pictured are now deceased, underlining why books such as this are so important to keep alive the memory of our 'Finest Hour' (courtesy Worcester News).

Afterword

Many outstanding personalities flew from and served in less glamorous roles at Duxford during the time preceding the Battle of Britain and the summer of 1940 itself. The most obvious, especially to the general public, is Douglas Bader, but to me personally, having studied Duxford's personnel extensively for twenty years, the most outstanding individual amongst this company of heroes was the quiet, intellectual and unassuming Brian Lane. Whilst Bader led through a mixture of high energy and swashbuckling arrogance, Lane was completely the opposite. That tough pre-war flight sergeant, George Unwin, remembered that:

> Brian was completely unflappable, no matter what the situation in the air. Someone would sight the enemy and shout excitedly over the R/T, only for Brian's calm acknowledging tone to settle everyone down, as if we were on a stroll in the park! He always made the right tactical decision, no matter how quickly this had to be decided. Although I was an NCO back then and Brian an officer, we became friends and were absolutely as one in the air.

It wasn't just his pilots, though, that Brian looked after, as Fred Roberts, an armourer, remembered:

> A lot of the officers were real snobs during the early days, but Brian Lane wasn't like that at all. He knew everyone under his command by their first name and had time for us all, no matter how lowly their rank.

His combat record, of eight enemy aircraft destroyed, also shows that he fully deserved the rating of 'exceptional'; as Frank Brinsden, a flying officer serving with Lane in 1938/40, said:

> Of course we of 19 Squadron, being in 12 Group, were engaged nowhere near as often as 11 Group's squadrons. Had Brian Lane commanded one of those squadrons his score would have been much higher, I am sure.

In June, 1941 the Duxford Sector was sorry to see Squadron Leader Lane go when he was given a staff appointment in the Middle East, indicating that his potential had been recognised.

Unfortunately the arid climate disagreed with him, so Brian returned home, attending a Spitfire refresher course before joining 167 'Gold Coast' Squadron as supernumerary, to gain up-to-date combat experience. On 13 December 1942, Squadron Leader Lane led a section of Spitfires on a low level sweep over the Dutch coast, seeking targets of opportunity. Two FW 190s intercepted the Spitfires, and Lane was never seen again. The record confirms that he was shot down into the North Sea by *Oberleutnant* Walter Leonhardt of 2/JG 1; Brian Lane remains missing to this day.

Brian Lane's story, and in particular his untimely fate, underlines the fact that war is neither a game nor an adventure. It is a tragic waste of young life.

In 1940, the Duxford Sector was a vital component in the System of Air Defence which saved this country from a Nazi invasion. All who served there at that time should be rightly proud of their achievement, which we must never forget – the day we do, the sacrifice of Brian Lane and those like him will have been in vain. Fortunately, today Duxford is owned by the Imperial War Museum and widely regarded as Europe's premier aviation museum, attracting thousands of visitors from all over the world every year. Long may that remain the case, for every visitor walks with the ghosts of 1940 on that hallowed ground.

Acknowledgements

The photographs in this book largely came from the personal albums of Duxford veterans or their relatives. I would like to thank them all, both living and deceased, for their kind help and friendship over the years.

Martin Woodhall, son of Group Captain EB 'Woody' Woodhall, kindly gave me permission many years ago to use extracts from his father's unpublished memoir, the Battle of Britain section of which appears in print here for the first time.

John Gillies sourced the 66 Squadron photographs, and Geoff Faulkner did likewise with those of 264. Thank you to you both.

Select Bibliography

Spitfire! The Experiences of a Fighter Pilot, S/L 'BJ Ellan' (Brian Lane), John Murray, 1942.

Spitfire Squadron, Dilip Sarkar, Air Research Publications, 1990.

Bader's Duxford Fighters: The Big Wing Controversy, Dilip Sarkar, Ramrod Publications, 1997.

Battle of Britain: Then & Now, Mk V, Edited by WG Ramsey, After the Battle, 1989.

Men of the Battle of Britain, Kenneth Wynn, Gliddon Books, 1989.

Reach for the Sky, Paul Brickhill, William Collins & Sons Ltd, 1954.